Egg Nog · Elves
"Oy Vey"

David Lloyd Strauss

Copyright © 2023 | Egg Nog Elves Oy Vey LLC

ISBN: 979-8-9857860-0-2

Version 11.23.2023 | November 2023

All rights reserved. No part of this publication may be reproduced, distributed, or transmitted in any form or by any means, including photocopying, recording, or other electronic or mechanical methods, without the prior written permission of the publisher, except in the case of brief quotations embodied in critical reviews and certain other non-commercial uses permitted by copyright law. For permission requests, reach out through davidstrauss.com

Egg Nog. Elves. Oy Vey. LLC
David Strauss
PO Box 28
Boulder, Colorado 80306

ORDERING INFORMATION:

Special discounts are available on quantity purchases by corporations, associations, and organizations. Contact the publisher at the above address for special discounts.

Energy Vampires is a Trademark of ENERGY VAMPIRES LLC
A Giggle Yoga Project Production
Published by Giggle Yoga LLC

Energy Vampire Series
Energy Vampire Holiday Series

I dedicate this book to my fellow mutant humans who seek out humor in difficult situations.

Table of Contents

WELCOME! 3

Holiday Whirlwind 5

Dreaming... of a Drama-Free 7

Egg Nog

Sip Your Way to Sanity! 11

A Conversation with Egg Nog 15

Elves

Elf Zen 19

Elf Wisdom 23

Oy Vey

The Secret Spell 29

The Joys of "Oy Vey" 31

The Zen of "Oy Vey" 37

Holiday Roundup

Pecan Pie & Matzoh Ball Soup 41

Family Drama Starring "Energy Vampires" 45

Gift Giving for 'Karen' and 'Joe' 55

Preparing for the Family "Fiesta" 61

Taming Holiday Expectations 65

Boundaries for the Emotional Minefield 69

Holiday Table Conversations 73

Festive Wisdom 76

Drama Reset Button 79

Post-Holiday Shenanigans 85

Table Game: "Elf Capers & Eggnog Elixirs" 93

David's Other Books 108

About the Author 112

Welcome...

Welcome to the world of holiday hilarity, where Egg Nog flows like a river of creamy calm, Elves are more than just toy-making maestros, and "Oy Vey" becomes the anthem for every eyebrow-raising moment. This isn't just a book; it's your secret map to navigating the festive labyrinth of family get-togethers, where energy vampires lurk around every mistletoe and laughter is your best defense.

As you turn these pages, prepare to embark on a knee-slapping journey as you are guided through the treacherous terrain of holiday gatherings, where Aunt Martha's critique of your life choices becomes as predictable as the appearance of fruitcake, and Uncle Joe's conspiracy theories are more colorful than the holiday lights.

But fear not! With a cup of Egg Nog in hand – spiced, spiked, or straight – you'll find solace in its nutmeg-infused wisdom. It's not just a festive drink; it's a symbol of inner peace amidst the chaos of clashing relatives and overcooked turkeys.

And let's not forget our pointy-eared allies, the Elves. These pint-sized Zen masters of holiday shenanigans are here to impart their 'Grin, Twinkle, Glide' philosophy. They're the silent ninjas in the corner, reminding you to keep your cool when the holiday heat rises.

"Oy Vey," the phrase that's music to your ears, will become your go-to mantra. It's your verbal eyeroll, the perfect response to every overcooked roast, every awkward conversation, and every surprise visit from those family members you 'forgot' to invite.

As for the energy vampires, those festive foes who thrive on drama and pessimism, you'll learn to tame them with humor, redirection, and maybe a strategically timed "Oy Vey." They're like the Scrooges of the season, but even Scrooges have their place at the table.

So, strap on your holiday boots, arm yourself with a sense of humor, and dive into a world where the holidays are an adventure to be savored, one laugh-out-loud moment at a time. Welcome to the ultimate guide to surviving – and thriving – in the holiday season. Let the festivities begin!

Holiday Whirlwind

◆ ◆ ◆

In the land of holiday cheer so bright,
Where eggnog flows through the festive night,
Mischievous elves craft their spells and play,
And "oy vey" moments surprise us along the way.
'Tis the season of joy, family near and far,
With gatherings aplenty, like twinkling star,
But in this package of holiday delight,
A touch of drama can take its flight.
Fear not, dear reader, for in your hand,
Lies a guide to help you understand,
"Eggnog, Elves, and Oy Vey" it's named,
For festive survival, it's been acclaimed.
Cheeky and insightful, this book's your key,
To survive the chaos with glee,
No more the family roast is the main course,
Or energy vampires, you'll fend off the most.

So, raise your glass of eggnog high,

And chuckle with elves as they fly,

With occasional "oy vey" in the mix,

Let's unwrap these tips, quick as a flick.

With this trusty guide in your grasp,

The holiday whirlwind, you'll clasp,

In laughter, love, and drama-free style,

Together, let's make the season worthwhile.

Dreaming... of a Drama-Free Holiday...

Imagine a dream world where holiday gatherings are as smooth as silk, where every family member, friend, and coworker is an angel, and dinner conversations and holiday parties are drama-free and delightful.

Now, wake up from that dream and brace yourself for the reality that awaits — a holiday season brimming with personal quirks, friendly banter, coworker capers, and yes, even your pets, who amusingly navigate the festive frenzy just as bewildered as you.

How do you stay calm, cool, and collected through the forest of quibbles that define our holiday celebrations? Uncle Bob's conspiracy theories, Cousin Corrin's endless complaining, Aunt Linda's health updates, and the never-ending sibling rivalry — they're all part of the package. Let's not forget the inappropriate political partisans and rambunctious religious banters.

With a sprinkle of humor and a dash of wisdom, "Egg Nog, Elves, and Oy Vey" is the perfect companion for those braving the festive season with family, friends, and foes in tow.

With your curiosity peaked, let's begin a journey filled with laughter, learning, and a generous serving of eggnog as we discover how to turn family feuds into fun, and chaos into cherished moments. After all, it's the mix of madness and love that makes holidays an adventure worth remembering.

Egg Nog

David Lloyd Strauss

Sip Your Way to Sanity!

Egg Nog, that delightful, creamy concoction is more than just a holiday beverage — it's the ultimate elixir for traversing the turbulent seas of holiday gatherings. Imagine it as your secret weapon, a velvety smooth superhero in a cup, ready to rescue you from the perils of family stress.

It's a clever companion in the lively dance of family interactions. Imagine it as your holiday ally, a comforting presence in your hand, offering a touch of joy and a clever way to navigate tricky conversations.

Picture this festive scene: You're amidst a lively family gathering, surrounded by twinkling lights and holiday cheer. Aunt Mildred, always full of surprising stories, and Cousin Cooper, ready to discuss the latest news, are both heading your way. Here, your cup of Egg Nog becomes more than just a treat; it turns into a strategic ally.

Let's set the scene: Aunt Mildred has cornered you, armed with unsolicited advice about everything from your love life to your career choices. Just as you feel the urge to dive into the nearest pile of coats, remember the Egg Nog. If you're too far away to get a fresh glass from the decanter, take a mental gulp of its calming, nutmeg-infused goodness. Feel the imaginary richness coat your insides, turning your sighs of frustration into sighs of creamy contentment. Egg Nog doesn't judge; Egg Nog understands.

And it's not just for Aunt Mildred's life coaching. When Cousin Cooper starts his annual rant about politics, or when Grandma interrogates you about when you're going to settle down and give her great-grandchildren, that's your cue. Pour yourself another glass of that sweet, eggy serenity. Each mental sip is a reminder that you're in the eye of the holiday storm, shielded by an invisible, delicious force field.

Remember, Egg Nog is versatile. It can be spiced, spiked, or sipped straight. Each variation offers a different level of mental fortification. Need a little extra courage to face Uncle Bob's dad jokes? Spike your Egg Nog with a shot of humor. Looking for patience to endure the family's new karaoke machine? Add a dash of cinnamon-spiced tolerance.

Egg Nog teaches us a valuable lesson: in the hurricane of holiday chaos. There's always a sweet, creamy haven to be found. So, when the going gets tough, and the conversations get tougher, take a deep breath and a big swig of Egg Nog. After all, it's the holidays — a time to savor the craziness, one soothing, mental sip at a time. Cheers to that!

Holding your Egg Nog is like having a little piece of holiday spirit in your hand. It's comforting and gives you something to focus on when conversations get overwhelming. It's like holding a little bit of holiday magic, providing a sense of calm amidst the buzz of family chatter.

In those moments when holiday conversations unexpectedly take a sharp turn, your cup of Egg Nog becomes an invaluable ally in maintaining composure. When they turn towards the less-than-merry, when you're taken aback by the direction of the dialogue but want to stay cool, calm, and collected, let your Egg Nog be your silent support.

Hold your Egg Nog cup high and politely ask to step away. With a friendly smile, you can gracefully say, "Excuse me, I'm just going to top up my Egg Nog." It's a simple, festive way to take a break, gather your thoughts, and return refreshed, ready to steer conversations toward more joyful topics.

If you can't gracefully step away, gently cradle your cup and take a thoughtful sip, allowing its smooth, creamy texture to help veil any immediate emotional reactions. This act of sipping Egg Nog grants you a moment to gather your thoughts and stabilize your emotions. While you do this, quietly say to yourself:

"Not my drama. Not my nonsense."

This simple mantra, coupled with the calming act of enjoying Egg Nog, can provide a brief respite, helping you to navigate the conversation with grace and avoid being drawn into the whirlpool of negativity.

So, at your next holiday party, remember that your cup of Egg Nog is more than just a delicious tradition—it's your festive aid in making the most of every merry moment.

David Lloyd Strauss

A Conversation with Egg Nog...

YOU: (Sighs and takes a sip of Egg Nog) You know, Egg Nog, I could really use some advice on dealing with Aunt Mildred and her unsolicited life coaching.

Egg Nog: (Chuckles) Ah, Aunt Mildred, the self-appointed guru of holiday gatherings! Well, my friend, when life gives you Aunt Mildred, make sure you've got your Egg Nog ready. Here's a little nugget of wisdom:

Nod · Sip · Dodge.

YOU: Nod, sip, and dodge? What's that all about?

Egg Nog: (Winks) It's simple. When Aunt Mildred starts dishing out advice on everything from your love life to your career choices, nod like you're listening intently. Give her the "Oh, you're so right" nod. Then, take a sip of me, let my creamy goodness soothe your nerves, and finally, dodge the conversation like a pro.

YOU: (Laughs) I like the sound of that! But what if she asks me directly about my life choices?

Egg Nog: Ah, the direct approach! Well, when that happens, take a bold sip of me, let my holiday magic infuse you with confidence, and then, hit her with a light-hearted deflecting comment. Something like, "You know, Aunt Mildred, I've been taking advice from an expert lately... my good friend, Egg Nog!" Trust me, it'll make her smile, and she might even change the subject.

YOU: (Grinning) Egg Nog, you're a lifesaver! What about Cousin Cooper's political rants? Those can be a real mood-killer.

Egg Nog: Ah, Cousin Cooper, the political pundit of the family! Well, my dear friend, when he starts going on his annual political tirade, take a generous sip of me. I'll infuse you with a dose of patience and understanding. Then, you can playfully tease him by saying something like, "Cousin Cooper, you should run for office with that passion!" It'll lighten the mood, and who knows, he might even chuckle and change the topic.

YOU: (Laughs) Egg Nog, you've got this all figured out! What if Grandma starts interrogating me about settling down?

Egg Nog: Ah, Grandma, the matchmaking maven! Well, my savvy companion, when Grandma starts her matchmaking mission, take a comforting sip of me. I'll wrap you in a warm, eggy embrace. Then, you can reply with, "Grandma, I've got my trusty Egg Nog here to keep me company for now. Who needs a partner when you've got creamy goodness?" It's a lighthearted way to let her know you're in no rush.

YOU: (Laughing) Egg Nog, you're not just a delicious drink; you're a family survival expert!

YOU: (Proudly) Why thank you! I've been through many holiday gatherings, and I've seen it all. Just remember, my friend, with a sip of me and a sprinkle of humor, you can navigate the trickiest of family conversations. Cheers to making the holidays a bit more merry, one sip at a time!

Elves

David Lloyd Strauss

Elf Zen

As the holiday season twinkles into life, there's a little elfin secret mantra to keeping your spirits bright.

"Grin, Twinkle, Glide!"

Imagine this: You're at the annual family holiday bash, the air buzzing with excitement, laughter, and the inevitable drama, and here comes Uncle Fred, gearing up for his notorious political rant, or Cousin Sarah, eager to share every detail of her latest dietary escapades. Instead of bracing for the usual stress, channel your inner holiday elf and embrace:

"Grin, Twinkle, Glide."

As you listen patiently, flash a grin as warm as the crackling fireplace, let your eyes twinkle with the joy of the season, and glide through the conversations with the effortless grace of a snowflake drifting through the winter sky.

When the conversation turns to the year's controversies or the latest family gossip, just remember to "Grin, Twinkle, Glide."

Let a warm, genuine grin spread across your face, reflecting the joy and warmth of the season. Let your eyes twinkle with the light of a thousand fairy lights, seeing the wonder and humor in every moment. And glide through each interaction with the elegance and ease of a figure skater on a frozen pond.

This isn't just a mantra; it's your ticket to a holiday season filled with laughter, lightness of heart, and a touch of elfish magic.

"Grin, Twinkle, Glide" is your silent, cheerful companion, your reminder that no matter the situation, you can always find joy and peace in the holiday spirit. It's like wrapping yourself in a cozy blanket of festive goodwill, where you're there to bask in the warmth of family and friends, not to debate or deliberate.

When you grin, it's your way of warmly accepting the swirl of conversations around you without judgment or expectations.

Twinkling is your quiet, joyful acknowledgment of the moment, much like the shimmer of ornaments on holiday decorations.

And gliding? That's you gracefully moving through the gathering, a serene spectator to the lively banter, content in simply savoring the presence of loved ones without engaging in the antics.

This holiday season, let "Grin, Twinkle, Glide" guide you to a place of peaceful enjoyment, where being together is the greatest gift.

When should you "Grin, Twinkle, Glide?"

In the midst of holiday gatherings, when a relative or friend starts to unload a sleigh full of negativity, let your imagination take you to a more playful, festive realm.

Visualize the speaker not as they are but as a charming elf straight from the heart of Santa's workshop. Picture them adorned with oversized, twinkling eyes, a comically long nose, and garbed in a kaleidoscope of festive colors as vivid as the Christmas lights adorning the tree.

As they speak, imagine each word accompanied by a parade of sparkling bubbles floating out of their mouth like tiny, joyous ornaments. This charming and humorous mental transformation turns their stream of negativity into a delightful, elfin spectacle, effectively lightening the emotional load of their words and breaking the spell of their seriousness. This imaginative escapade is more than a mere diversion; it's a festive shield, guarding your holiday cheer against the frost of negativity.

As you engage in this merry mental visualization, you'll feel the dreariness of their words melt away, their gloomy tone softened by your elfin imagery. The scene becomes less of a downpour of complaints and more of a playful dance of holiday bubbles, each popping away harmlessly in the air.

So, the next time you're caught in a blizzard of pessimism, let your mind transform the moment into a lighthearted holiday tableau. With this newfound imagery, the words of your personal 'Grinch' become as harmless and amusing as a frolic of elves, ensuring that your spirit stays as buoyant and bright as the star atop the Christmas tree.

Embrace this imaginative technique and keep your holiday season filled with mirth, laughter, and an unshakably festive spirit.

David Lloyd Strauss

Elf Wisdom

Now, let's delve into the enchanting world of elf wisdom. These joyful beings from the North Pole, known for their infectious laughter and kind hearts, offer us valuable lessons wrapped in the spirit of the season.

Like a cozy fireside story, each piece of elf wisdom is a guiding light through the lively maze of family gatherings, transforming potential challenges into moments of wonder and connection.

The Joy of Embracing the Unexpected

Picture an elf's delight when discovering an unexpected color on their palette of paint. Such is the joy found in the unforeseen twists of family gatherings. When Uncle Fred begins his annual political discourse, imagine it as an unexpected hue, adding to the rich mixture of family conversations. Greet it with a smile and a gentle shift to more cheerful topics, like a favorite holiday memory, turning the potential tension into a moment of shared nostalgia.

A Playful Heart in the Midst of Happiness

Elves never lose their sense of fun, even when the toy workshop is in full swing. This holiday let's channel this playful spirit. When Cousin Sarah takes center stage with her tales, sprinkle the conversation with light-hearted comments and funny stories. It's like an elf adding a dash of glitter to a toy, turning a mundane moment into something special, and bringing laughter to the table.

Cherishing Each Moment as a Precious Gift

Just as elves treasure every second as they craft toys for children, we can view each moment with our family as a precious gift. When Aunt Mildred starts her complaints, listen with an open heart, then gently steer her towards happier memories. It's like an elf turning a simple block of wood into a cherished toy, transforming everyday complaints into golden moments of shared joy.

Laughter as the Sparkle of the Season

In the elven world, laughter is as essential as the jingle of bells. When the holiday air becomes heavy with serious talk, let's lighten it with the sparkle of laughter. Share a funny holiday memory or a witty observation, much like an elf tossing a handful of sparkling snowflakes into the air and watch as the room lights up with smiles and joy.

The Elf's Dance Through the Workshop

Elves are masters of adaptation, skillfully moving from one task to another. Let's embrace this flexibility. When family plans change or unexpected guests arrive, dance through these changes with the grace of an elf, finding joy in the new and unexpected and turning every twist into a part of the holiday dance.

The Elf's Secret to Happiness

For elves, happiness is found in the simple acts of crafting and singing. This holiday let's find our joy in the simple things. Redirect dull conversations to the delights of the season — the gentle fall of snow outside, the sweet scent of baking treats — inviting everyone to share in the wonder of these simple pleasures.

The Elf's Gift to the World

Elves give selflessly, their hearts full of kindness. When we encounter family members who seem lost in their own worlds, let's offer them the gift of understanding and empathy, much like an elf bestowing a carefully crafted toy, bringing warmth and light to their hearts.

The Elf's Legacy

Elves create toys that become lasting memories for children. This holiday, let's create unforgettable moments with our family. Whether it's starting a new tradition or reviving an old one, these shared experiences weave the story of our holidays, turning each gathering into a cherished chapter in our family's history.

Let the wisdom of elves guide us this holiday season, turning each family gathering into a chapter filled with joy, laughter, and love. Like a beautifully illustrated holiday storybook, each piece of elf wisdom adds color, warmth, and magic to our festive celebrations, helping us navigate the season with a heart full of cheer and a spirit as light as a snowflake. Let these heartwarming lessons lead you through the festive season, turning every gathering into a magical holiday celebration.

Oy Vey

David Lloyd Strauss

The Secret Spell

With the delightful aroma of spiced apple cider and the melody of holiday tunes floating through the air, "Oy Vey" emerges as your secret spell to ward off the inevitable family drama.

Picture this: Aunt Martha, in her obnoxious holiday sweater, embarks on her annual critique of your career choices, or Uncle Joe, his eyes twinkling under the mistletoe, launches into his newest conspiracy theory. At these moments, "Oy Vey," steeped in rich Yiddish tradition, becomes your warm, chuckle-inducing hug amidst the holiday hullabaloo. It's your clever nod to the ridiculousness, a verbal twirl that lightens the mood with its humor and insightful perspective, much like a jingle bell's playful chime.

In the humming repertoire of family shenanigans, where laughter and light-hearted disputes mix like cookies and milk, "Oy Vey" is your cue to step back and view the scene through a lens of amusement and warmth. It's a gentle reminder that the essence of the holiday season isn't found in picture-perfect postcards but in the joyous, laughter-filled chaos of our wonderfully imperfect families.

So, as the holiday drama inevitably unfolds, let "Oy Vey" be your merry mantra, a symbol to cherish the little foibles and funny moments that make family gatherings so endearingly memorable. It's an invitation to find beauty and joy in the heartwarming spectacle of holiday togetherness, a reminder to embrace each quirky, heartfelt moment.

Let "Oy Vey" guide you through the festive season with laughter and love, celebrating the unique tapestry of your family's holiday traditions.

The Joys of "Oy Vey"

In the wild world of words and family drama, "Oy Vey" is your superhero. It's your secret weapon, your verbal confetti cannon, and your ticket to surviving the madness with a chuckle. If you haven't fully embraced the power of "Oy Vey," we're about to embark on an adventure into its wonder.

If there were a granddaddy of Yiddish expressions, "Oy Vey" would be king of the throne. Imagine it as the verbal equivalent of a facepalm, a sigh of epic proportions, or a melodramatic eye roll. Born in the heart of Jewish culture, "Oy Vey" has grown up to be the life of the party, transcending cultural boundaries like a linguistic globetrotter.

The Universal Emotion Decoder

During the holiday season, "Oy Vey" becomes your decoder ring for family gatherings. It's not just a phrase; it's your secret weapon for surviving the holiday circus. Aunt Agnes criticizing your holiday sweater? "Oy Vey" to the rescue! Cousin Jimmy's passionate plea for fruitcake rights? Cue the "Oy Vey" orchestra. It's like having a remote control for holiday chaos. Uncle Bob diving into conspiracy theories? "Oy Vey!" Your niece toppling the Christmas tree? "Oy Vey!" It's the magic wand that turns seasonal madness into a comedy show.

The Negativity Neutralizer

Now, let's uncover the real superpower of "Oy Vey" – its unmatched ability to neutralize negativity.

Imagine this: Cousin Carla is on a rampage about the candy cane shortage. What's your plan? You sprinkle in an "Oy Vey," and suddenly, the conversation does a 180-degree spin into hilarity. It's like using a laughter grenade to diffuse pessimism.

The Creative Conversation Juggler

"Oy Vey" isn't just a phrase; it's a playful pressure release valve.

Picture this classic holiday scene:

Uncle Fred: "Why don't you have a job yet?"

You: "Oy Vey, Uncle Fred, let me tell you my thrilling job search tales."

In a flash, you've turned the tables, and Uncle Fred is chuckling. It's like a magic trick that transforms awkwardness into amusement.

The Master of Family Alchemy

"Oy Vey" is the master of family alchemy. It brings folks together through shared sarcasm and laughter. When "Oy Vey" makes an entrance, it's like an invite to a stand-up comedy night. It says, "We're all in on the joke," or "Let's tackle this holiday madness together!" It's the secret handshake of satire that turns ordinary gatherings into uproarious spectacles.

The Universal Emotion

What makes "Oy Vey" truly magical is its universality. It's not confined to any specific context or emotion. Whether you're celebrating a triumph, commiserating over a mishap, or navigating the turbulent waters of a contentious family gathering, "Oy Vey" is your trusty companion.

The Art of Neutralizing Negativity

Now, let's unlock the secret behind "Oy Vey's" remarkable ability to neutralize negativity.

Picture this scenario: You're at a holiday gathering, and Aunt Susan starts a tirade about the weather, how it's too cold, or how it ruined her plans for the day. What do you do? Enter "Oy Vey." With a well-timed utterance of this phrase, you effortlessly acknowledge Aunt Susan's complaint while simultaneously diffusing her negative energy, bouncing the negativity right back and allowing you to carry on with holiday cheer.

The Quirky Deflection

"Oy Vey" isn't just a neutralizer; it's a deflection device. It takes the focus off the problem and turns it into a shared moment of levity. Take, for instance, the classic exchange:

Aunt G: "Ugh, I can't believe I burned the turkey!"

You: "Oy Vey, the turkey has seen better days. But remember that time we tried deep-frying it? Now, that was an adventure!"

In this scenario, "Oy Vey" acknowledges the mishap but swiftly redirects the conversation to a positive memory, allowing both parties to chuckle and move forward.

The Unifier

Another enchanting aspect of "Oy Vey" is its unifying power. It's a phrase that brings people together in a shared moment of empathy and humor. When someone uses "Oy Vey" in response to a challenge, it invites others to join in the camaraderie of life's absurdities. It says, "I've been there too," or "We're all in this together." This subtle connection strengthens bonds and helps to diffuse tense situations.

Imagine you're at a family barbecue, and Uncle Bob is recounting his latest lawn care mishap—how he mistook the weed trimmer for the lawnmower and created a grassy masterpiece that rivals the Amazon rainforest. With a hearty "Oy Vey" from the crowd, the entire gathering becomes a chorus of laughter and understanding. It's the great unifier, the reminder that life's blunders are the ties that bind us.

The Graceful Exit

"Oy Vey" also serves as an elegant way to bow out of a conversation or gracefully exit an uncomfortable discussion. If you find yourself entangled in a heated debate or caught in the crossfire of family drama, a well-placed "Oy Vey" can signal your desire to disengage without causing offense.

But "Oy Vey" isn't just a troubleshooter; it's a gracious exit strategy when conversations take an unexpected turn. Whether it's during a heated debate about the best pie filling or an impassioned discussion about the merits of artificial vs. real Christmas trees, a well-timed "Oy

Vey" can gracefully signal your desire to bow out without causing offense.

The Celebratory Chorus

But let's not forget that "Oy Vey" isn't just for deflecting negativity; it's equally potent in moments of celebration. When someone shares a joyous announcement, like a new job or an engagement, responding with "Oy Vey" adds a touch of humor and affection to the festivities. It's a way of saying, "I'm thrilled for you, and I'm here to share in your happiness."

"Oy Vey" in any Season"

Oy Vey" is not just a seasonal phrase; it's a linguistic Swiss Army knife, versatile and handy for all kinds of situations throughout the year. Whether your friend spills coffee on their pristine white shirt in the heat of July or your coworker grumbles about the never-ending thermostat wars in the office come spring, "Oy Vey" is your go-to response. Its true charm lies in its ability to neutralize negativity in any scenario.

When you hear a friend venting over their endless commute or a colleague groaning about office coffee rules, a timely "Oy Vey" not only acknowledges their frustration but also sprinkles in a dash of humor. It acts like a refreshing breeze on a sweltering day, gently reminding us that the little quirks and challenges of life are what bind us together, transcending seasons and reasons.

The Holiday Toastmaster

Now, let's toast to the versatility of "Oy Vey." It's not just for commiserating over holiday cooking mishaps; it's equally adept at celebrating life's victories. When your best friend shares the exciting news of their engagement, responding with a joyful "Oy Vey" adds a lighthearted touch to the merriment. It's a way of saying, "I'm overjoyed for you, and I'm here to share in your happiness."

"Oy Vey" All Year Long

"Oy Vey" is the phrase that makes every season brighter and every mishap more manageable. Its holiday magic extends to all facets of life, from summer picnics to autumn leaf-raking adventures. So, embrace its enchantment, and let "Oy Vey" be your year-round, holiday-inspired companion. May it add humor and grace to every moment, whether you're decking the halls or just navigating the beautiful chaos of everyday life. Oy Vey, what a wonderful phrase!

"Oy Vey" Unplugged

You're at a picnic in the park, and someone accidentally squishes the sandwich you spent ages crafting into a work of art. Your response? A melodious "Oy Vey!" It's not just a phrase; it's a symphony of understanding in the face of sandwich mishaps, and it's equally fitting when your coffee spills on your work shirt or your shoelaces refuse to cooperate on a Monday morning.

Deck the Halls with "Oy Vey"

Picture this: you're decorating the holiday tree, and that perfectly placed ornament slips from your grasp, crashing to the ground in a shower of glitter. What's your immediate response? A hearty "Oy Vey!" Of course! It's the phrase that encapsulates the holiday spirit—the good, the bad, and the glittery. It's the holiday anthem of resilience in the face of tinsel tangles and cookie catastrophes, or in the case of Chanukah, latke mishaps and menorah malfunctions.

The Zen of "Oy Vey"

In the wild jungle of family gatherings, where drama lurks around every corner, and conversations resemble a tangled web of chaos, there exists a hidden path to serenity known as "The Zen of Oy Vey."

This age-old wisdom passed down from wise holiday sages is your ticket to inner peace amidst the holiday storm. It's a mantra that transcends time and culture, a reminder that when negativity threatens to engulf you, you can remain the tranquil eye in the hurricane.

So, brace yourself as we quietly embark on a journey into the heart of "Oy Vey" enlightenment and explore the Zen-like art of countering holiday energy vampires with humor, grace, and a touch of silliness.

In the presence of family drama, take a deep breath and exhale with an 'Oy Vey' mantra to release tension.

When negativity flows like a river, be the bamboo that bends but does not break, and say, 'Oy Vey.'

In the art of mindful listening, let 'Oy Vey' be your anchor when navigating stormy conversations.

Embrace the wisdom of the Tao: 'Those who complain the most are often the most in need of compassion,' so respond with 'Oy Vey.'

Like a Zen master, cultivate patience and respond to complaints with 'Oy Vey,' knowing that this too shall pass.

In the realm of ancient wisdom, remember that the more you react, the more energy vampires feed on, so choose 'Oy Vey' as your response.

As Lao Tzu taught, 'Respond to anger with virtue and bitterness with 'Oy Vey,' for it diffuses the storm and invites harmony.'

When negativity seeks to disrupt your inner peace, channel your inner sage and respond with the mantra of 'Oy Vey.'

The art of the 'Oy Vey' smile: Like the Mona Lisa, it conveys mysterious amusement in the face of adversity.

In the great tapestry of life, weave the thread of 'Oy Vey' to navigate the complexities of family dynamics.

As Confucius said, 'He who understands the art of 'Oy Vey' understands the essence of wisdom.'

In the book of family gatherings, 'Oy Vey' is your chapter on resilience and composure.

Meditate on the sound of 'Oy Vey,' and let it be your inner mantra when faced with holiday challenges.

Like a Tai Chi master flowing with the energy, embrace 'Oy Vey' as your graceful response to family quirks.

In the Zen of holiday serenity, 'Oy Vey' reveals the path to inner calm.

Ancient wisdom teaches that the softest response can be the most powerful—thus, 'Oy Vey'.

When surrounded by chaos, adopt the 'Oy Vey' attitude as your secret to maintaining inner balance.

Confucius said, 'The superior person is calm in the midst of adversity, responding with 'Oy Vey' wisdom.

Channel your inner sage and let 'Oy Vey' be the mantra that transforms family friction into laughter.

In the spirit of yin and yang, 'Oy Vey' is the balancing force that neutralizes negativity during the holidays.

As the ancient proverb goes, 'He who masters 'Oy Vey' masters the art of living.'

In the realm of family harmony, the 'Oy Vey' mindset is your key to unlocking doors of understanding.

In the garden of family relationships, 'Oy Vey' is the mindful fertilizer that nurtures growth.

Embrace the 'Oy Vey' approach to bring serenity and humor into the midst of holiday turmoil.

As the sage of old would say, 'When the storm of complaints brews, let 'Oy Vey' be your gentle rain of wisdom.'

David Lloyd Strauss

Pecan Pie & Matzoh Ball Soup

With the holidays approaching like a runaway sleigh on a sugar high, you suddenly realize it's the night before the family festivities—an occasion that fills your heart with more mixed emotions than a holiday fruitcake.

Your excitement bubbles like a frothy cup of eggnog, ready to whisk you away on a sleigh ride of joy. You imagine the mouthwatering bouquet of your favorite dishes wafting from the kitchen. The savory aroma of roast turkey, the intoxicating scent of garlic mashed potatoes, and the sweet fragrance of Grandma's pecan pie, your absolute favorite, all blend together in a tantalizing symphony of flavors.

Ah, if you're fortunate enough during these holiday gatherings, you might find yourself being served a big, comforting bowl of matzoh ball soup. It's a dish that's almost as much a part of many family traditions as your chatty Aunt Martha and your conspiracy-theorist Uncle Joe.

Those deliciously fluffy matzoh balls, floating serenely in a nurturing chicken broth, are like edible hugs, warming you from the inside out. It's a dish that can make all the family drama seem a little more bearable, a reminder of the warmth and love that's at the heart of these festive occasions.

Back to Grandma's pecan pie, it's a culinary masterpiece, a dessert that transcends mere sweets and ventures into the realm of legend. It's the treat your grandchildren's grandchildren will remember. With a perfectly flaky crust that crumbles in your mouth like a snowflake's delicate touch, it's a buttery canvas upon which the star of the show, the pecan filling, takes center stage—not to mention the homemade whipped cream with a touch of Irish Crème.

But then, like a wayward snowball to the face, a thought strikes you. You can't help but remember the dramatic spectacle of last year—the unforgettable performance of Energy Vampires, those negative, nagging people and conversations that left you questioning whether you were at a family gathering, an audition for a soap opera, or had front-row seats to a circus.

It's like reliving an awkwardly hilarious sitcom episode, one where you felt caught between being embarrassed and utterly perplexed. "Am I really related to these people?" you might wonder as the memories of over-the-top disputes and cringe-worthy confrontations resurface.

As you prepare for the holiday gathering, you can't help but think, "Oy Vey, I know who's going to be there—the usual suspects." A chorus of complainers kvetching and critiquing anything and everything that has a hint of goodness. They come straight out of a made-for-movie, real-life comedy.

First up is Sister Sue, the family's reigning Complain-o-Matic, who can turn any topic into a whining session. From the weather to the mashed potatoes, she's got a gripe for every occasion. Then there's brother Broo, the Master of Nitpicking, who never met a detail he didn't want to dissect. His specialty? Finding flaws in even the most flawless plans.

Antie Anjie, the Drama Diva, is always ready to steal the spotlight with her tales of woe and misfortune. From stubbing her toe to running out of whipped cream, no setback is too small to warrant a dramatic monologue.

And let's not forget Uncle Bunkle, the Sarcasm Sultan, whose jokes are legendary for their groan-inducing punchlines. He's armed with verbal darts, tossing one-liner insults and judgments that pierce your soul like a dagger to the heart of a vampire. None are safe from his wit.

But amidst the cast of colorful complainers, there are the Family Saviors, the unsung heroes of holiday gatherings, who strive to bring peace and harmony to the festive chaos. Mom and Dad, the dynamic duo of diplomacy, are on a mission to keep everyone in check with their soothing words of reason and an endless supply of hugs, not to mention the not-so-subtle elbow jabs to your ribs when it's best to keep your mouth shut.

And then, there's Grandma Gerda, the Pie Connoisseur, whose sweet treats have the miraculous power to put a smile on even the grumpiest face. Her made-from-scratch dreamy deserts are the ultimate peace offering, and her secret ingredient might just be a sprinkle of magic and "Oy Vey."

Grandpa Grins, who believes he's the world's best storyteller, steps in with his quirky tales that transport everyone to far-off lands and bring a sense of wonder to the table. His stories have the power to captivate even the most ardent complainers, turning their attention from grievances to the magic of imagination.

So, as you stand on the precipice of another family gathering, remember that you're not alone in this holiday rollercoaster. The energy vampires may try to drain your festive spirit, but you have a secret weapon—your very own family saviors, armed with humor, love, and a pinch of magic to keep the holiday drama at bay.

With their help, and armed with Egg Nog, Elves, and Oy Vey, you're ready to navigate the twists and turns of this festive season and make it a memorable, laughter-filled adventure.

Now, let's unmask the holiday Energy Vampires.

Family Drama
— Starring —
"Energy Vampires"

Hold onto your hats because behind this holiday curtain lie characters that could give Shakespeare a run for his money. We're talking about the Energy Vampires, those drama-loving masters of misery who can turn your festive season into an award-winning soap opera.

It's time to pull the velvet rope, raise the drapes, and introduce you to the cast of Energy Vampires that could rival the nutcrackers in eccentricity. These are the relatives, friends, coworkers, or inner voices that can suck the holiday spirit out of you faster than you can say, "Oy Vey."

As we unmask these Holiday Energy Vampires, imagine eggnog in one hand, an elf on your shoulder whispering "Grin, Twinkle, Glide," and an occasional "Oy Vey" to give you comedic relief.

Here we go...

Tinsel-Takers (a.k.a. Narcissists)

These holiday thieves have a unique ability to turn every conversation into a one-person show starring themselves. Whether you're discussing gift ideas, holiday plans, or your latest gingerbread house masterpiece, they somehow manage to redirect the spotlight squarely onto their achievements, desires, and grand adventures.

Here's how it may go down...

Imagine this scene: You're sitting at the dinner table, sipping your eggnog, and casually mentioning your plan to volunteer at a local shelter during the holidays. And then, boom, they chime in with, "Oh, that's cute! But you know, let me tell you about this one time when I volunteered in this remote village in Antarctica, saving penguins and even teaching them to waltz."

Or picture this: You're indulging in some delicious homemade cookies, sharing your family's tradition, and they jump in with, "Baking? Well, that's interesting. I actually have my own line of gourmet holiday treats. You know, Martha Stewart herself personally requested my secret recipe."

And just as you're enjoying a cozy chat about classic holiday movies, they can't resist interjecting, "Speaking of movies, I had my moment in the spotlight once. I starred in a holiday blockbuster, and the critics were raving about how I outshone the entire cast."

Yep, those are the Tinsel-Takers for you, always ready to one-up any holiday conversation, even at the dinner table!

Merry Mayhem Makers (a.k.a. Drama Queens)

If you are looking for someone who has a knack for transforming even the simplest mishap into a full-blown theatrical extravaganza, these are your people. Whether it's a case of misplaced wrapping paper or a minor cooking mishap, they have a remarkable talent for turning these everyday incidents into epic blockbuster sagas that demand immediate attention and, of course, heaps of validation and sympathy.

Does this sound familiar…?

Imagine this: they drop a delicate glass ornament, and it's like witnessing a Shakespearean tragedy unfold before your eyes. They start wailing dramatically as if it's an omen of impending doom. You can't help but wonder if they've mistaken your living room for a theater—stage lights and all.

Now picture this: a minor kitchen mishap occurs, and suddenly, the burnt pie crust becomes a culinary catastrophe of historic magnitude. They're shedding melodramatic tears and declaring their culinary incompetence as if they were auditioning for a reality cooking show. It's like watching a Food Network cooking disaster episode come to life in your very own home.

And then there's the minor disagreement with a relative. It's not just a simple disagreement; it's an all-out heated argument where they take on the role of the tragic hero. There are passionate monologues bellowing unfairness, over-the-top gestures, and enough dramatic flair to make you think you've stumbled into a Shakespearean play rather than a family holiday gathering.

The Festive Faux-Friends (a.k.a. Wannabes)

These holiday chameleons strive to fit in by adopting the interests and preferences of those around them. Whether it's a sudden passion for snowboarding or a newfound love for knitting, they enthusiastically embrace whatever they perceive as the latest trend or popular activity.

Have you ever seen one of these…

Imagine being at a holiday gathering and suddenly encountering these chameleonic characters. They're the ones who strive to fit in by adopting the interests and preferences of those around them, like social butterflies in search of the perfect pollen. You mention your love for classic holiday music, and like a holiday DJ, they quickly declare it their favorite genre, despite never having mentioned it before. It's as if they've unearthed their long-lost love for Bing Crosby overnight.

Then, a family member shares their passion for collecting vintage holiday decorations, and the next day, the Wannabe shows up with a collection of their own, claiming it's always been a cherished hobby. It's like they have a magical closet full of vintage ornaments that only comes out during the holiday season. And just when you discuss your enthusiasm for a particular holiday recipe, they suddenly claim to be a culinary expert in that very dish, offering unsolicited tips and advice as if they've been crafting it since birth. It's like they have a culinary diploma hidden up their holiday sweater sleeves.

These Wannabes are like human chameleons, ready to blend into any holiday environment, but their adaptability sometimes leaves you wondering if they even have their own identity. So, prepare yourself for their ever-changing interests and sudden expertise in whatever the holiday conversation topic du jour may be.

The Grinches in the Gathering (a.k.a. Crabs in a Pot)

These holiday party poopers are the self-appointed guardians of gloom, armed with a universal "Thou Shalt Not Have Fun" decree. Whenever someone dares share a moment of success or joy, they swoop in faster than Santa on a jet-powered sleigh, ready to serve up a hearty helping of a reality check with a side of pessimism. It's as if they have a toll-free hotline to the International Grinch headquarters, always on call to pull others down to their level of disdain.

Picture this: you're eagerly sharing your promotion at work with your friends and family, and the room is ready to erupt in applause. But wait, there's the Grinch in the corner, looking like they've just sucked on a lemon. Instead of celebrating with you, they launch into a lecture on pessimism. It's as if they've taken a masterclass in raincloud creation and graduated with honors in buzzkill studies.

Now, imagine a family member excitedly revealing their impressive weight loss journey. The atmosphere is positively electric with positivity, and everyone's ready to join in the celebration. But not the Grinch. Oh no, they step in with their expert analysis like they've got a PhD in dampening spirits. They insist that maintaining that weight loss is about as likely as finding a unicorn in your backyard. Their comments are like a wet blanket on a bonfire of happiness.

And then there's your creative triumph—those handmade holiday decorations you've proudly displayed. Your eyes twinkle with the joy of creation, but here comes the Grinch with their unsolicited verdict: your decorations won't survive the next season. It's as if they have a crystal ball specifically for predicting the lifespan of your tinsel and baubles. They're like the ghost of holiday decor yet to come, warning of impending obsolescence.

Grumble Guru (a.k.a. The Constant Complainer)

Now, let's talk about the Constant Complainer, shall we? These fine folks have taken the noble art of complaining and turned it into their life's masterpiece. It's as if they've taken on the mission to catalog every inconvenience and discomfort that exists during the holidays and present it to you in glorious detail.

Picture this: the room temperature is set to what most consider comfortable. But for the Constant Complainer, it's akin to surviving the Sahara or the Arctic. They'll regale you with tales of thermostat wars and dramatic accounts of feeling like they're either melting into a puddle of goo or freezing into a human popsicle.

Now, let's move on to the holiday tunes. While the majority are bopping to the beat and getting into the spirit, the Constant Complainer will have none of it. Every song selection is met with a furrowed brow and a litany of complaints. "Too cheerful," they'll declare. "Too melancholy," they'll grumble. It's as if they have a degree in holiday music criticism.

And when the feast is served, even if it's a culinary masterpiece that deserves its own Food Network show, the Constant Complainer will find a way to pour a bucket of complaints over it. From the seasoning on the turkey to the choice of side dishes, they'll dissect each culinary element with the precision of a master chef critiquing a Michelin-star meal. Bon appétit, indeed!

The Never Satisfied (a.k.a. Perpetual Disdain)

Ah, the Never Satisfied crew, our perpetual seekers of more, better, and different. They're like holiday treasure hunters, but instead of gold doubloons, they're after something even more elusive: the ever-elusive "perfection."

Picture this scenario: you've spent weeks hunting down the ultimate holiday gift, something that would make even Santa's elves envious. You're brimming with excitement as they unwrap it, only to be met with a lukewarm response. "It's nice," they say, their voice dripping with mild disappointment. "But I thought it would be something more... extraordinary." You can't help but wonder if they were secretly hoping for a surprise visit from a unicorn.

Now, let's talk about the holiday feast. It's a culinary spectacle, a gastronomic masterpiece with flavors that dance like sugarplum fairies on your taste buds. But for the Never Satisfied crew, each bite is an opportunity for critique. "This is good," they'll declare, "but it could use a touch more seasoning." It's as if they've morphed into culinary experts overnight, channeling their inner Gordon Ramsay.

And when it comes to holiday decorations, they'll size up your festive efforts with a critical eye. No matter how many lights, tinsel, or ornaments you've painstakingly placed, they'll suggest that you should have gone for a more extravagant display. In their world, no amount of holiday bling will ever be enough to satisfy their insatiable appetite for more.

Party Pooper Extraordinaire. (a.k.a. "I Don't Want to Be Here")

These people have mastered the art of turning any festive gathering into a somber affair with the flick of a metaphorical switch. It's as if they've been handed the official responsibility of dampening everyone's spirits.

Imagine this scenario: the room is alive with laughter, and everyone is enjoying the holiday merriment. But here comes the Joy Destroyer, wearing a perpetual scowl and emitting an aura of gloom that could rival the darkest winter night. They make it clear that they'd rather be anywhere else, and they're not afraid to show it.

Now, let's talk about gift-giving. You've put thought and effort into selecting the perfect present for them, but when they unwrap it, their enthusiasm rivals that of a sloth on a lazy Sunday afternoon. "Oh, another gift," they sigh, as if your carefully chosen offering were a mere inconvenience. You can't help but wonder if they secretly wished for coal.

And when it's time for holiday games and activities, the Joy Destroyer is the first to protest. Board games? Too boring. Carol singing? Too cheesy. Even a friendly snowball fight is met with disdain. Their mission? To spread their anti-festive agenda far and wide, like the Grinch's sour attitude but without the eventual heartwarming transformation.

There you have it, the triumvirate of Holiday Energy Vampires: The Constant Complainer, The Never Satisfied, and the "I Don't Want to Be Here" Joy Destroyer. May your festive gatherings be blessed with an absence of these merry mischief-makers!

Your Inner Grinch (a.k.a. The Pesky Inner-Vampire)

Watch out because lurking within you is a sneaky little vampire! It's that relentless voice that insists you're not quite up to snuff, the gloomy cloud of self-doubt that can rain on your parade, and the impulse to indulge in junk food while simultaneously critiquing your physique. This inner fiend is the master of turning unresolved anger inward, playing a solo blame game, and hosting never-ending pity parties with you as the star guest. Your Inner Vampire might just be the sneakiest of them all, quietly draining your mojo with its negative thoughts and bad habits.

This tiny beast that fancies itself as the Grinch in a Santa suit is the drama queens of your psyche, always seeking the spotlight and stealing the show with their incessant self-doubt and gloomy predictions. They're the ultimate masters of disguise, cunningly convincing us that we're never good enough, that our holiday efforts are as effective as trying to wrap presents with a hyperactive kitten, and that we'll never measure up to our own expectations.

Here's how your Inner Vampire plays hide-n-seek with your psyche.

You finally land at the family gathering like a jet on a wet, icy runway, bracing for all the possibilities of what may be said by the unfiltered conversations. Words are flowing like gravy and Uncle Bob's critiques are as abundant as fruitcakes. His unsolicited life advice lands with all the grace of a flying reindeer crashing into your self-esteem. Your inner vampire perks up, ready to feast on your self-doubt like a hungry gingerbread man. "Perhaps he's right," it whispers sinisterly. "Am I really the poster child for poor decisions?"

But hold onto your marbles because your self-worth is not the main course tonight. Instead, channel your inner elf and remind yourself that Uncle Bob's words are about as valuable as a lump of coal in your holiday stocking. Take a deep breath, put on your best fake smile, and retort, "Well, Uncle Bob, pursuing my dreams feels like a sleigh ride through a blizzard of possibilities!" It may not look like I'm making decisions, but hey, I'm in the game and taking risks. Your inner vampire just got served a plate of holiday humility. You've brushed off his negativity like snowflakes on a snowman's shoulder.

Then there's Aunt Carol, reigning supreme as the queen of backhanded compliments. Her words flow like a river, sparkling on the surface but concealing hidden currents of criticism. She excels at making you question your life choices with her expertly timed remarks. Your inner vampire stirs, eager to feast on self-doubt like a hungry gingerbread person. "Could Aunt Carol be onto something?" it taunts. "Perhaps I'm not clever enough to dream big and carve my path."

But you catch yourself and slap that Inner Vampire voice silly. You channel your inner elf, adjust your holiday hat, and remind yourself that her words hold as much weight as a hobo dishing up tips on how to run a five-star restaurant. Take a deep breath, flash a brilliantly fake smile, and retort, "Well, Aunt Carol, even though it might look like I'm wading through a tangle of holiday lights, I'm savoring the adventure! My choices may not always align with the norm, but every one of my dreams deserve a shot at becoming true." Your inner vampire? It just got a hearty serving of holiday humility, brushed off like powdered sugar from a freshly baked cookie. You've transformed Aunt Carol's negativity into a festive lesson in self-confidence.

So, during those family gatherings when words are sharper than a candy cane swordfight, remember to catch yourself and get centered. It's not about you; it's about reveling in the holiday spirit, eggnog, elves, and all!

FREE
ENERGY VAMPIRE Detection Kit
DOWNLOAD

davidstrauss.com/free-energy-vampire-detection-kit/

David Lloyd Strauss

Gift Giving for 'Karen' and 'Joe'

The hilarious conundrum of picking out gifts for those wonderfully particular people in your life. You know the type—they can spot a flaw from a mile away and turn any gift into a masterclass in critique. But hey, we've got a plan that's as cheeky as it gets.

Instead of tiptoeing around their high standards, we're going to dive headfirst into the world of humor. We're talking about gifts that'll have them giggling at their own quirks and idiosyncrasies. Of course, we'll sneak in a genuinely thoughtful gem or two, just to keep things exciting. So, no more dilly-dallying—let's embark on a gift-giving adventure that'll have even the pickiest recipients grinning from ear to ear.

Here are some creative and cheeky gift ideas for those high-maintenance and complaint-prone self-proclaimed celebrities:

Custom Complaint Merchandise

Turn their grumbles into fashion statements with personalized T-shirts and coffee mugs featuring their most common complaints. Who knew complaining could be so stylish?

Gag Gifts Galore

Get ready to tickle their high-maintenance funny bone with a "Portable Complainer's Kit." It's got a tiny megaphone and a booklet of common complaints – the ultimate toolkit for a professional grumbler.

The "VIP Experience" Certificate'

Elevate their self-importance with a VIP experience certificate. It's like rolling out the red carpet for their high standards, literally!

Customized Complaint Journal

Help them document their daily grievances in style with a customized journal. From "Today's Epic Complaint" to "How I Elevated My Standards," it's a diary worth complaining about.

"Complaints of the Year" Award

Make their complaints legendary by declaring them the "Complaints of the Year" winner. It's a prestigious honor for the most discerning complainer.

Personalized "High-Maintenance" Robe

Give them a robe fit for royalty, complete with the word "High-Maintenance" embroidered proudly. Now they can lounge regally while complaining comfortably.

"The Great Expectations" Board Game

Challenge their high expectations with a custom board game. It's like Monopoly, but instead of properties, they collect grievances.

Comedy Show Tickets

Treat them to a night of comedy where comedians roast high-maintenance quirks. It's a show where laughter trumps complaints.

Customized "Queen/King of Complainers" Crown

Crown them the reigning monarch of complaints with a regal headpiece. It's the perfect accessory for a royal complainer. Craft a regal crown with their title, "Queen/King of Complainers," as the centerpiece. It's a fun accessory for holiday gatherings.

"The Ultimate High-Maintenance Survival Kit"

Prepare them for any high-maintenance emergency with a survival kit featuring a mirror, hairbrush, and mini perfume. Because even emergencies should meet their standards.

These gifts strike a perfect balance between poking fun at their quirks and celebrating their unique qualities, ensuring they laugh while feeling appreciated and cherished during the holiday season.

David Lloyd Strauss

Preparing for the Family "Fiesta"

Buckle up because we're diving headfirst into the family fiesta, where energy vampires roam free! To ensure you're not the one getting sucked into their negativity vortex, here are ten cheeky tips to keep the festive spirit alive:

The Vampire Hit List

Start by creating a Vampire Hit List. Jot down the names of the energy vampires that are invited to the family shindig. Categorize them based on their unique complaints. Are they Tinsel-Takers, Merry Mayhem Makers, Blame-Blitzers, Festive Faux-Friends, Grinches in the Gathering, or Inner Ebenezers?

Counter-Complaint Arsenal

Craft clever responses to their classic complaints. Think of it as your secret stash of complaint kryptonite. These responses should be so good they'll have them second-guessing their own complaints.

Comic Relief

When deploying your responses, sprinkle in some humor. A well-timed joke can turn a complaint into a chuckle, and who doesn't love a good laugh?

Listen and Breathe

Remember to practice your active listening skills. Sometimes, all they need is a willing ear. Acknowledge their complaints, then gently redirect the conversation.

Divert and Conquer

Prepare a list of captivating topics to steer their thoughts away from complaints. Engage them in discussions that tickle their fancy.

Positivity Perks

Encourage positivity by rewarding it. When an energy vampire manages to keep their complaints at bay, give 'em a high-five or a piece of candy. Positive reinforcement at its finest.

Task Tailoring

If possible, assign them tasks that align with their interests. Keeping them occupied with something they enjoy can lessen the complaining.

No-Complaint Zones

Designate specific areas or times as "No-Complaint Zones." Get creative with your enforcement—maybe a silly dance or a kazoo fanfare for violators?

Lead with a Grin

Finally, lead by example. Show 'em how it's done with your infectious positivity. Your cheerful vibes might just be the cure for their vampire tendencies.

Armed with these tips, you'll be the master of ceremonies at the family fiesta, keeping those energy vampires in check and the holiday spirit soaring high.

David Lloyd Strauss

Taming Holiday Expectations

The enchanting game of taming holiday expectations, where we embrace the sparkle and spirit of the season without the weight of perfection on our shoulders.

Picture this: a holiday where the only expectation is to enjoy the twinkling lights and the warmth of shared smiles, a place where we swap out meticulous plans for spontaneous laughter and genuine connections.

It's about finding joy in the impromptu snowball fights, relishing the imperfectly wrapped presents, and savoring the slightly burnt cookies.

Let's unwrap the secrets to a holiday filled with cheer, minus the pressure. Imagine holding a magical wand that transforms your holiday expectations into a dance of delight and wonder.

So, grab a cup of egg not, snuggle up in your coziest blanket, and let's journey together into the heart of a truly merry and light holiday season!

Now, let's talk about the unspoken mantra of the holidays:

"No expectations, no disappointments"

It's like the Jedi mind trick for a stress-free festive season. Here's your guide to mastering the art of managing holiday expectations.

Embrace the Holiday Plot Twists

Imagine your holiday plans are a blockbuster movie, but instead of a predictable plot, expect the unexpected. Your cousin might turn up with a surprise pet llama, and that's the kind of holiday twist you'll cherish forever.

Be the Yoga Master of Plans

Your meticulously crafted schedule? Yeah, that's just a rough draft. Be as flexible as a gymnast at the Olympics. Plans may change, and that's where the adventure begins.

Perfectly Imperfect is Perfect

Your holiday might not look like a Martha Stewart magazine spread, but those mishaps and quirks are what will make it memorable. Who needs perfection when you've got character?

Spontaneity Adds Spice

Leave room for spontaneity because the best holiday stories start with, "We didn't plan for this, but..." Be open to the magic of the unexpected and, if you're feeling a bit spicey, be the unexpected.

Detox Your Expectations

Give those high expectations a well-deserved detox. Instead of obsessing over what should be, focus on what is. That's where the real beauty lies.

Families Are Like Snowflakes

Families, like snowflakes, are all unique. Adjust your expectations when it comes to family gatherings. There might be a few icy patches, but it's all part of the fun.

The Joy of Giving

Shift your focus from "What's in it for me?" to "What can I give?" The delight of giving can outshine any present under the tree. It's the thought that counts, not the price tag.

Mindful Munching

Practice mindfulness during the holidays. Take a moment to savor the flavors of your favorite dishes or enjoy the warmth of a cozy fire. Life's little moments are the ones that matter most.

Believe in the Magic

Last but not least, remember the magic. It might not be as visible as Santa's sleigh, but it's there—in the twinkle of fairy lights, the sound of laughter, and the warmth of togetherness. Embrace the Energy Vampires: Alright, folks, let's face it – those energy vampires are as predictable as holiday fruitcake. Don't hold your breath waiting for a miracle personality makeover. Instead, arm yourself with an "oy vey" and a dash of humor.

Prepare for Complaints

Brace yourselves for the incoming complaints because, trust me, they're as certain as mistletoe at a holiday party. Tinsel-Takers will boast, Mayhem Makers will stir the pot, and Blame-Blitzers will be ready to point fingers. Expect it and have your witty comebacks ready.

Celebrate Imperfections

Repeat after me, folks: "Perfection is overrated!" The holiday season isn't about everything going off without a hitch. It's about the quirky imperfections that make each gathering a unique adventure. So, don't sweat the small stuff; celebrate it.

Enjoy the Little Moments

Amidst the chaos, don't forget to relish the tiny pockets of holiday magic. Take a moment to savor that scrumptious gingerbread cookie, cherish a heartwarming conversation, and bask in the warm glow of twinkling holiday lights.

Keep Your Elf on the Shoulder

Picture a mischievous holiday elf perched on your shoulder, armed with a sly grin and a knack for keeping it real. Let this imaginary friend be your guide, reminding you to take things in stride, laugh at the absurdities, and navigate family dynamics with a hefty dose of acceptance and humor.

Boundaries for the Emotional Minefield

When Cousin Complainer starts inching too close, invading your personal space like you're a shelf for a holiday clearance sale, it's time to unleash your boundary-setting prowess. So, dust off your superhero cape (invisible, of course) because here's how to establish those oh-so-crucial healthy boundaries with a side of holiday zest:

The Forcefield of Personal Space

Imagine a hula hoop but make it magical and invisible. This is your personal space forcefield, and no one crosses it without a VIP pass. If Cousin Carol attempts a personal bubble invasion, execute the sidestep maneuver like a boundary ninja.

The "No" Shield

No" isn't just a word; it's a symphony of self-preservation. Practice saying it with a symphonic flourish, turning down Aunt Mildred's fifteenth invitation to join the fruitcake appreciation club. Instead, offer to lead a spontaneous dance-off in the living room.

Exit Strategies, Oscar-Worthy

You need an exit plan that would make Hollywood proud. When Uncle Fred launches into an impassioned monologue on the virtues of fruitcake quality, you'll be the stealthy evacuee who urgently needs to "check the football scores."

The Buddy System

Find a fellow boundary enthusiast – your partner in crime prevention. Stick together like secret agents on a mission, using subtle signals and nods to communicate your need for a covert rescue operation.

Phone, Your Stealthy Squire

Your phone isn't just a device; it's your covert ally. Sneak away for a strategic phone call with "Elf Command" or watch a video of penguin tap-dancing – return refreshed and ready to face the holiday brigade.

The Art of "I" Statements

When establishing your boundaries, employ the art of "I" statements with a flourish. Swap out "You're driving me nuts" for "I could use a moment of tranquility," demonstrating the finesse of a seasoned diplomat.

Time Limits for Family Olympics

Set time limits for your family interactions. When you can feel your patience dwindling faster than a melting snowman in July, employ your escape plan. It might involve a fictional cranberry sauce emergency.

The Power Seat

Claim your spot, the throne of the holiday kingdom. Whether it's the esteemed head of the table or the cozy fireside nook, choose your battlefield wisely – it's your personal domain for the day.

Master the Art of Diversion

Divert like a maestro. If Grandpa Joe's questions start resembling an interrogation, skillfully shift the conversation to topics like holiday fashion or the best way to decorate sugar cookies.

Your Self-Care Oasis

Designate a self-care sanctuary. Create a cozy corner with a good book, a warm blanket, and a secret stash of chocolate. Sneak away for moments of rejuvenation as needed.

Boundaries aren't barricades; they're bridges to healthier interactions. By asserting and respecting these boundaries, you'll make your holiday family gatherings a more enjoyable experience for all. So, go forth, boundary-setter extraordinaire, and may your personal space remain as sacred as the holiday cookie jar.

David Lloyd Strauss

Egg Nog · Elves · Oy Vey

Holiday Table Conversations

T he holiday table, where conversations can turn as frosty as an ice-cold candy cane faster than you can say, "Pass the gravy." But worry not. You're about to become the conversation maestro, adept at redirecting negative chatter and keeping the holiday spirit alive. So, grab your conversational magic wand, and let's wave away those downer discussions and keep the holiday harmony.

Dessert Delight

When Aunt Grumble starts complaining about the dessert selection, sweeten the talk with, "I can't decide which dessert is my favorite. What's your go-to holiday treat?"

Recipe Trance

As Cousin Cronnie dives into critique mode about the holiday dishes, stir up conversation with, "These recipes have such rich histories. Does anyone have a favorite holiday recipe handed down through generations?"

The Redirect and Relate

When a complainer starts on a negative tangent, redirect the chatter and say, "Oy Vey, I totally get what you mean. But speaking of positive surprises, remember that time we all found hidden treasure during a family scavenger hunt? That was such a plot twist!" Of course, with a spin of your own story.

Holiday Hilarity

When Negative Ned starts predicting doom for the future, turn the conversation into a comedy show: "Speaking of predictions, who can come up with the silliest New Year's resolution?"

The Humorous Deflection

When faced with a persistent complainer, lighten the mood by saying, "Oy Vey, that does sound challenging. But hey, who's up for a friendly game of holiday charades? It's the perfect way to keep the good vibes flowing and avoid a drama overdose!"

Festive Favorites

When Negative Nancy starts lamenting, ask about holiday favorites:

"Speaking of odd weather, does anyone have a favorite holiday tradition that's a bit unconventional?"

Odd and Outlandish

When Whiny Wilma dives into a gloomy prediction, steer the conversation to the peculiar and fantastical: "Predictions can be wild! Who has the most bizarre holiday story?"

The Joyful Juxtaposition

If someone brings up a gloomy topic, try this: "Oy Vey, I hear you, but let's flip the script. What's your all-time favorite holiday memory? Mine has to be that epic snowball fight that left us all in stitches—and not from complaints!"

Dream Discussion

When Grouchy Greta starts dreading the future, guide the chat toward aspirations: "The future is a blank canvas. What's one dream or goal you'd like to chase in the coming year?"

Gratitude Galore

As Mr. Complaint lists all the negatives, introduce some positivity: "Let's shift the focus. What's one thing you're thankful for, no matter how small, this holiday season?"

Kindness and Compliments

If someone resorts to personal attacks or insults, counter with compliments: "Speaking of being incredible, I've always admired your [positive trait]."

Humor as a Shield

When faced with personal attacks, deflect with humor: "I must have a target on my back today! Who else has had some friendly fire for me?"

Festive Wisdom

As the holiday season wraps us in its glittering embrace, let's sprinkle a dash of festive wisdom into our celebrations. It's a time to wear a smile as bright as the twinkling lights, to nod in understanding like an old friend, and to appreciate the unique quirks that each family member brings to the table.

Let's refrain from judging the burnt cookies or the mismatched gift wrapping; instead, let's accept every imperfection with the warmth of a crackling fire. Allowing each moment to unfold in its own merry way, we create a tapestry of memories woven with laughter, love, and a hearty dose of holiday cheer. Remember, it's not about creating the perfect holiday, but about cherishing the perfectly imperfect moments that make the season truly magical.

In this carousel of holiday cheer, let's also remember the art of gentle acceptance. As the festive tunes play and the aroma of holiday treats fills the air, embrace the diverse tapestry of personalities around you. From the enthusiastic storytellers to the quiet observers, every character adds a unique color to the holiday palette.

With each indulgent sip of eggnog and every shared chuckle, let's acknowledge the beauty in our differences, fostering a space where everyone feels valued and heard. This season, let our hearts be as open as the skies on a clear winter night, welcoming each experience with the joyous spirit of the holidays.

In doing so, we not only celebrate the season but also the wonderful array of souls that enrich our lives, making each holiday gathering not just an event, but a treasure trove of joyful moments.

David Lloyd Strauss

Drama Reset Button

You're navigating the high seas of holiday drama, sailing through a storm of family bickering, when suddenly, you spot it: the legendary "Holiday Drama Reset Button." This isn't just any button; it's a shining beacon of hope, adorned with twinkling lights, mistletoe, and a big red candy button.

With a deep breath, you reach out and smack it with all the gusto of a child unwrapping their first holiday gift. Instantly, the room transforms! Aunt Martha's critique of your career choices turns into enthusiastic cheers for your daring choices. Uncle Joe's conspiracy theories morph into heartwarming tales of past family adventures. And those energy vampires? They're now toasting with glasses of Egg Nog, their complaints drowned out by jolly elfin laughter. As the button works its magic, you lean back, a triumphant grin on your face, watching the holiday chaos reset to a scene of festive harmony and joy, just like a scene from the jolliest holiday movie ever.

Navigating Political Patter

To navigate this culinary minefield, adopt the strategy of a festive ninja. When Aunt Martha launches her political meatballs across the table, dodge them with a twirl and a grin, offering a tantalizing distraction: "Speaking of change, have you tried these amazing stuffed mushrooms? Revolutionary flavor!" Remember, the key to surviving the political platter is to keep your humor saucy and your responses sweeter.

Sleigh Ride Redirect

When Cousin Joe starts carving into party policies as he carves the turkey, raise your glass for a toast: "Here's to family, food, and the mysterious disappearance of all political talk under the mistletoe!"

Elfin Humor

Insert a light joke. "I bet even Santa steers clear of politics to keep his ho-ho-ho in top shape!"

Boundary Baubles

Politely say, "Let's keep the holiday spirit bright and politics-free," with a smile as warm as a cup of cocoa.

Listening by the Fireside, show respect and interest in their beliefs as if sharing tales around a cozy fire, without the need to agree or argue.

Financial Chatter Cheer

Gift of Non-comparison
Steer away from money matters; instead, discuss the joy of handmade gifts or the beauty of holiday decorations.

Material-free Merriment
Focus on enjoying each other's company, sharing stories, and playing holiday games.

Wise Winter Words
If financial topics arise, offer general, non-personal advice or anecdotes, keeping the mood light.

Countering the Holiday Energy Vampires

Tinsel-Taker's Tale Twist
When a narcissistic relative starts monopolizing the conversation, turn it into a festive game. "Wow, that's an epic story! Let's make it more fun – everyone gets a turn to add an outlandish twist to it. I'll start: the turkey gains superpowers!"

Grumble Guru's Giggle Game
When faced with a relentless complainer, introduce a bit of humor. "Every time you find something to grumble about, we all have to laugh or make a funny face. It's the new holiday rule!"

Festive Faux-Friend's Flattery Fiesta
When a wannabe jumps on every bandwagon, challenge them with exaggerated flattery. "Oh, you love holiday music too? You must be the secret composer of all these classic carols!"

Pessimist's Positivity Potion
For that always-negative relative, create an imaginary potion. "You sound like you need a sip of the Positivity Potion. It magically turns

every complaint into a compliment!"

Doubter's Delightful Dare

When faced with a skeptic, dare them to find joy. "I bet you can't go an entire hour only saying positive things. If you do, you win the Golden Elf Award!"

Grinch's Glitter Grenade

When faced with a holiday Grinch, sprinkle some festive cheer their way. "I hear your concerns, but have you seen the sparkle on these new holiday lights? It's like a disco ball exploded in here!"

Eggnog Empathy Elixir

Combat the gloomy Gus with a dose of creamy understanding. "You seem upset about the pie not being perfect. Let's add an extra splash of rum to the eggnog and call it even, shall we?"

Tinsel-Talker's Turnaround

When a relative hogs the conversation, redirect it with holiday flair. "That's an interesting story about your trip, but let's pass the tinsel microphone around. What's everyone's most hilarious holiday mishap?"

Yuletide Yoda's Wisdom Whisper

Offer sage advice wrapped in holiday spirit. "The turkey may be burnt, but remember, as the Yuletide Yoda says, 'Perfection, the enemy of good, it is.'"

Santa's Sleigh Strategy

When someone tries to steer the conversation off course, take the reins like Santa himself. "Hold on to your reindeer! Before we dive into politics, let's go around the table and share what we'd ask Santa for this year - the sillier, the better!"

FREE
ENERGY VAMPIRE Detection Kit
DOWNLOAD

davidstrauss.com/free-energy-vampire-detection-kit

David Lloyd Strauss

Table Game
"Elf Capers & Eggnog Elixirs"

Objective

Navigate through impromptu holiday scenarios and challenges using creativity, humor, and a touch of elfin charm.

Number of Players

Any number (ideal for family gatherings)

Materials Needed

Tableware (spoons, forks, napkins, etc.) as game pieces. A "Magic Eggnog Cup" (any cup or glass designated as the game's special item).

How to Play the Game

Each player starts with one piece of tableware in front of them. It can be a fork, knife, spoon, napkin, really, anything from the table.

The Magic Eggnog Cup

Place the designated "Magic Eggnog Cup" in the center of the table. This cup serves as the game's centerpiece and can be 'awarded' to players during the game.

Starting the Game

The youngest player starts the game. They pick a player and pose a fun, holiday-themed scenario or challenge. For example, "If you were an elf, how would you use a spoon to solve Santa's sleigh breakdown?"

Responding

The chosen player must come up with a creative and humorous response using the piece of tableware in front of them. They have 30 seconds to answer.

Judging

After the response, other players at the table can show their approval or disapproval by either clapping or gently tapping their tableware. High approval wins the player the "Magic Eggnog Cup."

Passing the Turn

The player who just responded picks the next player and poses a different scenario or challenge, continuing the game.

Using the Magic Eggnog Cup

If a player wins the "Magic Eggnog Cup," they can use it once to skip their turn, pass a challenge to another player, or create a new rule for one round (e.g., every answer must rhyme).

Game End

The game continues until everyone decides to end it, or when dessert is served. There's no formal point system – the aim is to have fun and be creative.

Benefits

- Encourages family members to interact and laugh together.
- Sparks creativity and quick thinking.
- Inclusive and easy to play for all ages.
- No preparation is needed; uses everyday items.

This game is designed to be flexible and spontaneous, making it perfect for lively holiday dinner conversations. It brings the charm of elves, the spirit of egg nog, and the humor of "Oy Vey" moments to your family gathering.

David Lloyd Strauss

Post-Holiday Shenanigans

Elf-Inspired Unwinding Tricks

The holidays have whooshed by like a snowstorm, and now it's time to follow in the tiny footsteps of our festive friends – the elves. Picture them trading in their toy-making tools for fluffy slippers and lounging caps, engaging in their quirky post-holiday traditions.

The Relaxing Nog-Tail

Mix up a rejuvenating Egg Nog concoction the elf-approved way. Add a pinch of cinnamon, a dollop of honey, and a splash of relaxation. As you sip, envision each drop melting away the holiday frenzy.

Egg Nog Aromatherapy

Who says Egg Nog is just for drinking? Elves love filling their space with the comforting aroma of this holiday staple. Light an egg-nog scented candle and let the sweet, soothing scent envelop you in calmness.

Embracing 'Oy Vey' as a Relaxation Mantra

Post-holiday, let "Oy Vey" be your humorous cue to decompress. Each time you find a stray decoration or untangle a string of lights, laugh it off with an "Oy Vey" and a shrug.

Entertainment, Elf-Style

Elves are experts at finding joy in the simple things:

Comedy Night In: Elves adore laughter. Host an evening where you share funny holiday stories or watch a comedy. Laughter is the best medicine, especially after intense festivities.

Crafting Capers: Elves never really stop crafting. Engage in a light-hearted craft activity, like making a silly photo frame for your funniest holiday picture.

Nature's Nurturing Naps

Following an elf's advice, take a walk in the hushed, wintry outdoors. Then, snuggle up for a nap in a cozy nook, wrapped in the warm embrace of blankets and sweet dreams of elfin escapades.

Chill Tunes: Elves' Secret to Serenity

Elves know the power of music. Compile a playlist of mellow melodies to fill your home with harmonious vibes. Let the music flow like a gentle river, carrying away the remnants of holiday chaos.

◆ ◆ ◆

In true elf fashion, remember: "When the holiday uproar subsides, it's time for some merry and bright downtime!" Wrap yourself in the comforts of Egg Nog indulgences, elfin relaxation rituals, and the lighthearted release of "Oy Vey." Here's to a post-festivity period brimming with laughter, rest, and a generous dose of whimsy.

Happy unwinding!

David Lloyd Strauss

Bedtime Story

Once upon a chilly December night, in the heart of the North Pole, Egg Nog, Elves, and Oy Vey gathered around a crackling campfire. The stars shimmered overhead, and a gentle snowfall painted the world in a serene blanket of white.

Egg Nog, the creamy and comforting one, spoke first. "You know," he said, swirling in his cup, "I've always been the go-to drink when things get frosty, just like dealing with those energy vampire relatives during the holidays."

Elves, mischievous and playful, chimed in, "Ah, Egg Nog, you're the embodiment of holiday cheer! When things go awry, I always remember to embrace your spirit and find joy in the festivities."

Oy Vey, wise and full of Yiddish humor, nodded knowingly. "Indeed, my friends. But how do you handle the 'Oy Vey' moments when Aunt Edna starts her annual rant about the state of the world?"

Egg Nog chuckled softly. "Well, I've found that when Aunt Edna begins her 'Oy Vey' symphony, I take a slow sip and let her have the stage. It's her moment to shine, and I just enjoy the show."

The Elves grinned mischievously. "You're onto something, Egg Nog. Just like when we turn mishaps into memorable pranks, we can turn 'Oy Vey' moments into shared laughter."

Oy Vey raised an eyebrow. "But what about those Blame-Blitzers and Tinsel-Takers who always find someone or something to blame for their 'Oy Vey' moments?"

Egg Nog, his eggnog cup now adorned with a miniature detective's hat, replied, "Ah, Oy Vey, my friend. When they start pointing fingers, I say, 'Let's investigate this together.' We turn their blame game into a fun holiday mystery!"

Elves eagerly joined in, "And while they're busy solving mysteries, we sneak off to enjoy some holiday mischief, just like we do when we're supposed to be wrapping presents."

Oy Vey laughed heartily. "You Elves and your tricks! But what about those moments when you can't escape the drama—when the energy vampires just won't quit?"

Egg Nog offered a warm smile. "Well, in those times, I've found that a sip of Egg Nog can help you keep your cool, like a cozy fireplace in the midst of a snowstorm."

Elves nodded in agreement. "And if all else fails, we break into a spontaneous holiday dance. It's hard to be a Grinch when you're dancing the Nutcracker!"

Oy Vey sighed with contentment. "You two certainly know how to handle the holiday chaos. I've learned a lot tonight. Remember, when in doubt, just mutter 'Oy Vey' with a grin, and watch your stress float away like snowflakes on the wind."

As the campfire crackled and the snow continued to fall, Egg Nog, Elves, and Oy Vey shared stories and laughter deep into the night. They knew that with a cup of holiday cheer, a sprinkle of mischief, and a dash of humor, they could navigate any family gathering with grace, even when the energy vampires we

And so, under the starry Arctic sky, they toasted to the magic of the season, with Egg Nog, Elves, and Oy Vey as their guides, ensuring that every 'Oy Vey' moment would be transformed into a joyful memory of holiday delight.

David Lloyd Strauss

Jokes for the Holiday Table

Ridiculous Jokes, but why not?!

(1) Why don't energy vampires like Egg Nog? Because they can't handle the spice of family gatherings!

(2) What do you call an elf who's good at calming family drama? A peace-keeper in pointy shoes!

(3) Why did the holiday dinner guest bring a ladder? To reach the high expectations at the table!

(4)   What's an elf's favorite part of a keyboard? The "escape" key, for when family drama starts.

(5)   Why did the Egg Nog cross the road? To avoid Aunt Mildred's unsolicited advice!

(6)   What do you call an elf who loves debates? A jolly good fellow with an argumentative twist.

(7)   Why was the energy vampire banned from holiday parties? Too draining on the festive spirit!

(8)   What's an elf's favorite exercise? Dodging family drama!

(9)   How does Egg Nog keep cool during the holidays? By chilling with the ice-cold relatives.

(10) Why did the elf refuse to play cards with the family? Too many jokers at the table.

(11) Why don't energy vampires like "Oy Vey"? It's too much light for their dark moods!

(12) What do you call a gathering of energy vampires? A draining experience!

(13) How did the elf fix the tense holiday dinner? With a little "elfin" magic and a lot of Egg Nog!

(14) Why was the energy vampire always lost? They could never find the "light" of the conversation.

(15) Why did the elf bring a map to the family gathering? To navigate through the emotional minefield.

(16) Why don't elves get caught in family drama? They always know how to "elf" their way out.

(17) How do energy vampires spice up their holiday meals? With a dash of negativity!

(18) Why did the elf start a yoga class? To teach relatives how to "bend" in conversations.

(19) Why did the Egg Nog hide in the fridge? To cool off from the heated family debates.

(20) What do you call an elf with a therapist degree? A family gathering survival expert.

(21) Why was the holiday dinner like a soap opera? Because of the extra serving of family drama!

(22) How do you know if an energy vampire's at your holiday party? The lights dim every time they talk!

(23) Why did the elf bring earplugs to dinner? To tune out the "Grinchy" complaints.

(24) Why did the elf start a band? To "drum" out the sound of family bickering.

(25) What's an elf's favorite holiday drink? "Oy Vey" on the rocks, to smooth out family gatherings.

(26) Why did the elf use a megaphone at the family dinner? To amplify the holiday cheer over the drama!

(27) How does Egg Nog avoid family arguments? It just mixes well with everyone.

(28) Why are energy vampires bad at gift exchanges? They always take more than they give!

(29) What's an elf's favorite game at family gatherings? "Dodge the Drama"!

(30) Why did the elf bring a stopwatch to dinner? To time how long it takes for the first "Oy Vey" moment!

(31) How does an elf keep its cool? By standing next to the family's snowman!

(32) Why don't energy vampires need watches? They always know when it's time to suck the fun out!

(33) What did the elf say to the stressed-out host? "Keep calm and tinsel on!"

(34) Why did the energy vampire get invited to the holiday party? To turn the lights down and the drama up!

(35) How do you make an energy vampire leave a party? Turn on the holiday spirit!

(36) What's an elf's favorite dance at family gatherings? The "Side-Step the Drama" shuffle.

(37) Why did the elf go to holiday parties? To spread cheer and steer clear of fear!

(38) What's an energy vampire's least favorite holiday song? "Joy to the World!"

(39) Why did the elf bring a joke book to the holiday dinner? To break the ice before Aunt Mildred does!

(40) How does Egg Nog keep conversations light? By whipping up some frothy topics!

(41) Why did the elf bring a shield to the family dinner? To deflect the drama arrows!

(42) What's an energy vampire's favorite holiday activity? Turning light-hearted chats into heavy debates.

(43) Why did the elf start a holiday podcast? To broadcast ways to escape family drama!

(44) How do you keep an energy vampire away from your holiday feast? Serve a plate of positivity!

(45) What's the elf's strategy for a peaceful dinner? Sit between the two most "chilled" relatives.

(46) Why did the elf bring a compass to the holiday party? To navigate through the sea of opinions.

(47) How does an elf mediate family arguments? With a sprinkle of humor and a dash of wisdom.

(48) Why are energy vampires bad at making toasts? They always roast before they toast!

(49) What's an elf's favorite mantra at family gatherings? "Peace on Earth and mercy mild, keep me away from the family wild!"

(50) Why did the elf bring a yoga mat to Christmas dinner? To stay flexible in tight situations!

David Lloyd Strauss

Acknowledgments

As I sit here, sipping my cup of eggnog and pondering the magical holiday journey that led to the creation of this book, I can't help but chuckle and feel immense gratitude. This whirlwind of a project wouldn't have been possible without the support and inspiration from a sleigh-load of amazing people.

First and foremost, a jolly shoutout to my coaches and mentors, the real-life elves of wisdom and wit who give me the insight and inspiration to continuously do what I love to do—create inspiring content. You have been the Santa's helpers in my writing workshop, guiding my sleigh through the blizzard of doubts and creative snowdrifts. Your support has been like the perfect blend of spices in my eggnog – just the right amount of zest and warmth to keep me going.

To the many Yoda's of humor in the most unlikely places, thank you for showing me the light side of dealing with Energy Vampires. You've taught me that laughter can be a powerful garlic necklace to ward off the doom and gloom.

And the coaches of everyday life, oh wise ones, who always reminded me that "Oy Vey" is not just a phrase but a perspective. You turned my grumbles into giggles, and my eye rolls into exclamations of wonder. You're the one who taught me that every family gathering could be a sitcom episode if you look at it the right way.

To my fellow giggle yogis, who have laughed with me (and at me) through every iteration of this book, your infectious laughter was the best soundtrack for this writing adventure. You've proven that the best way to spread Christmas cheer is laughing loud for all to hear!

A special elf hat tip to the squad of holiday cheerleaders in my life – you know who you are. Your encouragement was the sprinkle of cinnamon on the frothy top of my festive endeavors.

And of course, to the countless Energy Vampires I've encountered over the years – thank you for the inspiration. You've taught me that even the Grinch-iest of moments can be transformed into stories that bring joy, laughter, and a bit of mischief.

As we wrap up, I raise my glass of eggnog high. Here's to all the laughs, the facepalms, and the moments of elf-like mischief that brought this book to life. May your holidays be merry, your spirits bright, and your family gatherings free of drama (or at least full of the funny kind).

Cheers and Chuckles,

David Lloyd Strauss

To my early fans who pre-ordered this book...
BIG LOVE to you for your support!

Denise Wilkins

Marilyn Harpin

Judy Rutty

Lauri English

Nancy Spano

Mary Wodehouse

Kristi Allred Gall

Sharmoon Merritt

Clubhouse Fans

Special cheers to my fans and followers on the Clubhouse app. You gave my voice a home to launch this punny book.

Special Friends in Alphabetical Order

Alan Sizmur
Amanda Strauss
Angela Fox
Avry Stroeve
Autumn Riddle
Autumn Sette
Barb Wade
Bill Lamphere Jr.
Bobby Straus
Cathrin Strauss
Clinto Sistrunk
Denise Shannon
Devin Scott
Diane Uzelac
Diane Meekin
Dirk Schultz
Dorothy Steele
Drew Juen
Ed Scherzer
Eric Wright
Ethan Jones
James McCutcheon

Jesse Wright
Jey Lawrence
Jon Troshynski
Josh Wyles
Juliette Strauss
Kelly DeJoy
Kelly Straeter
Kent Schmetpecker
Kristi Allred Gall
Kyler Graff
Lee Brewer
Lee Zeller
Lori Stai
Marilyn Harpin
Maritane Joseph
Mary Lynn Wilkin
Mary Wodehouse
Matt Christou
Matthew Wood
Melissa Estes
Michael Cordova
Michael Weiner

David Lloyd Strauss

Mike Delsart
Mimi Newstadt
Nancy & Phil Mitchell
Nancy Fairchild
Nate & Laura Auffort
Phil & Nancy Mitchell
Ray & Rachel Bowers
Ryan Miller
Ryan Wipf
Sandy Brown
Scott Peterson
Shila Russell
Sol Salcedo

Stella Termin
Steve & Laura Allmen
Steve Borg
Susan Viebrock
Tara Sindylek
Tony Calucci
Trisha Rue
Valerie Watson
William Berry
Valerie Watson
Veronica Atkins
Yasmin Martinez

To my mother & Father,
and my two dogs,
Finnley & Giggles

BIG LOVE to all of you!

LOVED THIS BOOK?

Share on social media!

#EggNogElfBook
#EggNogElfOyVey
#DavidLloydStrauss
#EnergyVampires
Tell Your Friends! Oy Vey!

David's Other Books

David's 1st Book

David's 2nd Book

David's 3rd Book

David's 4th Book

About the Author

When a falling rock collided with David's head while exploring ancient ruins, his 5-year recovery became his life's purpose.

DAVID...

A results Coach with a Story of Thrills, Resilience, and Transformation. David's life reads like an adventurous novel, filled with twists and turns that shaped him into the transformational author, coach, mentor, and Life Strategist he is today.

From Tragedy to Triumph

At just 15, David's world crumbled with the death of his mother. Facing life alone as a runaway at that young age, he summoned a relentless spirit that propelled him through high school, college at CU Boulder, and into a world of boundless exploration.

THE ROCKFALL
A Brush with Death, A Gift of Destiny

While exploring ancient ruins, a falling rock struck David's head. The rockfall was a defining moment that created the opportunity for David to reinvent himself, beginning with those daring moments at ground zero of his collision with the rock. This incredible journey has forged his philosophy as a thought leader.

Scaling Heights, Diving Depths

David's zeal for life extends to scaling the 23,000-foot summit of Aconcagua, Argentina, plunging into the depths with SCUBA, and taking leaps from planes and bridges through skydiving and bungee jumping. His adventurous pursuits are metaphors for his Life Coaching philosophy: Embrace life fearlessly.

Philanthropist And Community Volunteer

David's world travel and philanthropic endeavors reveal a man who seeks to elevate humanity. His community service and world outreach resonate with his commitment to personal growth and social impact.

Begin Your Journey
With David's Coaching and Mentoring

David's unique approach is grounded in his own transformative experiences. He doesn't just talk about change; he embodies it.

From the rocky terrains to the soaring skies, from the personal hardships to global outreach, David's life is a testament to resilience, adventure, and love for people. His smile and energy invite you to join him on this remarkable journey.

Learn More...
CONNECT NOW!
DavidStrauss.com

Touch a Rock, Touch the Past
Touch a Flower, Touch the Present Moment.
Touch a Heart, Touch Eternity.

~ David Lloyd Strauss

Egg Nog · Elves · Oy Vey
Holiday Energy Vampire Series

www.ingramcontent.com/pod-product-compliance
Lightning Source LLC
Chambersburg PA
CBHW040315170426
43196CB00020B/2934